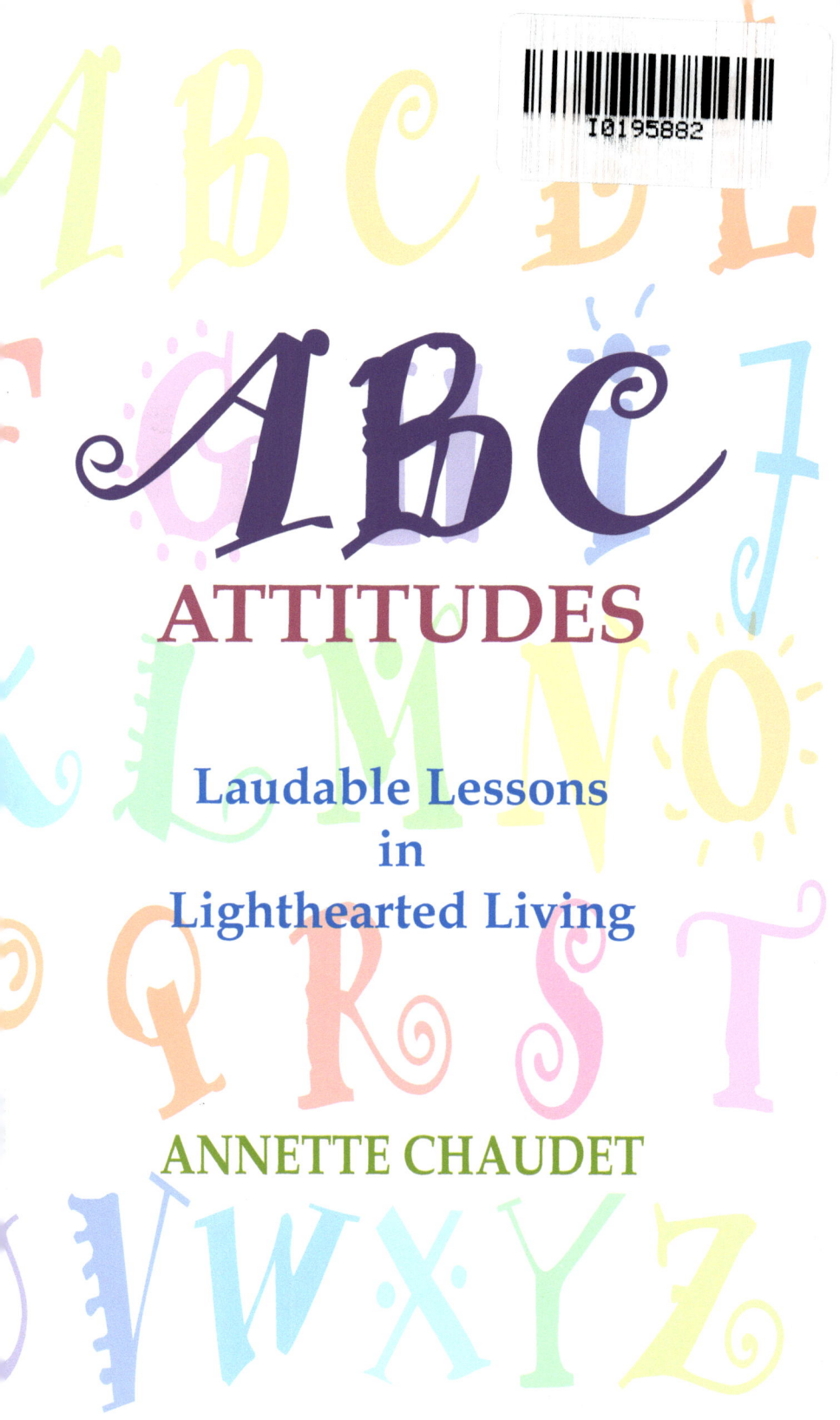

ABC
ATTITUDES

Laudable Lessons
in
Lighthearted Living

ANNETTE CHAUDET

Copyright 2012 Annette Chaudet

ISBN# 978-1-932636-77-2 Softcover

All rights reserved.
No part of this book may be reproduced or transmitted in any form or by any means, electronic or mechanical, including photocopying, recording or by any information storage and retrieval system without written permission from the publisher.

Book Design: Antelope Design

www.pronghornpress.org

Frequently Forgetting Fun we Fail to Find Favorable Fortune in Each Event, Easily Eliminating Ecstacy.

This Tome Tries To Tactfully Testify To the Necessity of Neatly Nurturing Novel Natural Celebrations of Certain Colorful Ceremonies Guaranteed to Gently Generate Genuine Gladness.

So, Sit Softly, Settle Sedately and Start Seeking Satisfaction, Slowly Savoring Silly Samples of Learned Lessons in Lighthearted Living.

Laugh Loudly!

Amuse Anyone with Acute Anecdotes And Achieve An Air of Authority Amid Anarchy.

Appoint Apprentices Anxious to Admire All Accomplishments And Afford Adequate Acclaim Among Apathetic Associates.

Ameliorate Abrasive Antagonistic Attacks And Attest to Affirmative Actions.

Acquire Albacore, Anchovies, Antipasto And An Appetite!

Amble Amok Among Asters And Apply Attention to Autobiographical Anthologies.

Appreciate Accurate Adaptations of Absurd Articles And An Affinity for Ambitious Achievements.

Admit Anger and Apologize, Abandoning All Adherence to Archaic Attitudes.

Appear Aflutter And Abashed About Always Angering Abominable Ancestors.

Avoid Accordions.

Bamboozle Baroque Bluenoses with Bawdy Boisterous Brilliant Banter.

Beseech Brethren to Bespeak Beauty, Boosting Beatific Behavior.

Bounce Boldly Blithe and Barefoot Beyond Big Burgeoning Bougainvillaea, Baffling Brainless Bullies.

Balance Blessings and Blights Because Blame Blackens Basic Bounty.

Begin to Be a *Bona fide* Benefactor.

Banish Bellyaching, Boredom and *Bêtes Noire* and Begin Boosting Bacchus.

Be Brave, Bring Back Benign Beneficial Business and Begin Being Brimful of Bliss.

Behold the Breeze, Balancing Brandy, Byron, Beethoven and Books.

Ban Bagpipes.

Cultivate Charm and Culture with Care and Consideration.

Constrain Careless Conversation and Covet Contemplation.

Consider a Cartwheel, a Carousel and a Concert, Cheerfully Challenging Companions to Caper in Charming Camaraderie.

Champion Cosmic Conservation, Calmly Concentrating on Candid Cooperation.

Communicate Concisely and Coherently, Captivating Company with Compassion and Character.

Command Charity Cordially, Consciously Countering Cantankerous Conflict.

Cut Colorful Cloth, Creating a Cloak of Cinnabar Chenille, a Chapeau of Cobalt Chambray and a Caftan of Cerulean Challis and Compare to Classic Couture.

Consistently Counsel Constraint in Conservative Civil Company but Choose Conspicuous Caprice in the Country.

Celebrate Cellos.

Demonstrate a Deep Desire to Define Dignified Demeanor.

Depart Downtown Directly, Drifting Dilatorily, Discretely Deigning to Drop Dephiniums Daffodils, Dahlias, Daisies, and Dandelions as you Drive.

Dream of Docile Dragons and Delirious Doves Disporting Dizzily with the Dalai Lama.

Decorate your Domicile with a Diptych Depicting Diminutive Dotted Dalmatians and Dashing Debonair Dragoons.

Declare Dauntless Dedication to Decent Decisions.

Decline Disharmonious Discussion, Dismiss Difficulties and Disagree with Dissenters.

Design a Dress of Dark Delft Denim and Dazzle your Detractors in Doubleknits.

Develop a Dossier of Desirable Dealings, Duplicate and Disseminate.

Disdain Drums.

Eagerly Engage the Enterprise (to Ease Evading Extraterrestrials) and Establish Embassies Everywhere.

Enjoy Exceeding Expectations and Evoke Echoes with Ease, Embracing Exceptional Episodes.

Eliminate Ego and Enlighten Everyone, Encouraging Ecstacy and Earnest Endeavors.

Enchant, Enthrall and Edify with Excellent Etiquette.

Experience Eagles, Egrets, Emus and Egypt Easily Eschewing Enervation.

Enumerate Enigmas and Eulogize Eclipses, Easily Enlivening Entire Evenings.

Enhance and Embellish Every Ensemble with Emerald Eyelet, Educing Eloquent Explanations.

Endorse Epicures and Experiment with Enormous Edible Encounters.

Ennoble English horns.

Forego Fussing, Forbid Frowning and Forge Forward into the Flow.

Foster Fondness for Friends, Flora and Fauna Facilitating Fellowship.

Ferret out Fabulous Fiery Fiestas and Flout a Fine Fandango Forthwith.

Festoon a Fedora, Fez and Fichu with Fabulous Fanciful Flame Flounces and Frantically Fling Forget-me-nots.

Forsake False Faith and Favor Fanciful Felines, Fairies and Flaubert.

Follow Farewells with Fine French Food and Fragile Fragrant Flowers.

Fly Free in Fustian Formation, Finding Favor with Fortune.

Formulate Fashion with Flair and Flummox Fastidious Fakes.

Favor French horns.

Gather Game Genies and Generate Goodwill Galore Gratis.

Guard Gentle Griffins and Gauche Greenhorns with Grace.

Gurgle with Glee and Give Gourmet Gifts to Grateful Goddesses, Glorifying Generosity.

Grasping Golden Gladiolus and Garnet Geraniums, Gaily Gambol on Green Grass

Gape at Gaugin, Giggle at Gulliver and Greet Gandhi Graciously.

Go Grab a Guru and Get Glad.

Gesture Grandly, Guaranteeing Greatness.

Greet Grumps with a Grand Gossamer Glissade.

Gag Glockenspiels.

Honor Hercules, Handel and Homer.

Hoard Heirlooms, Hawks and Holidays.

Hanker for Heliotrope Hosiery and Humble Hyacinths.

Howl Heartily, Hinting at Habitforming Hulas and Habañeras.

Happily Hone a Handful of Haikus.

Hurl Hocus-pocus Hard at Half-Hearted Hauteur.

Hail Heroes and Help Herons.

Hesitate to Handle History Heedfully.

Hype Harmonicas.

Impeach Inconsiderate Idiots.

Imagine Ibsen in Iberia Initiating Immodest Ideas.

Introduce Igloos, Icicles and Ice to Inquisitive Iguanas.

Impersonate Illustrious Impresarios and Influence Intense Idols.

Incarnate as Inexhaustible Industrialists and Intervene in Infamous Injustice.

Invite Invisible Iroquois to Informal Idylls.

Imbue Icons with Innocent Imperfections.

Indulge Irreverent Incantations to Illustrate Illusion.

Include Instruments.

Jog Jauntily Juggling a Jar of Jam.

Jest Joyfully in Japanese.

Juxtapose Juvenile Jinns and Jocund Jockeys.

Jumble Jaguars and Jackdaws; Just don't Jar the Japonica in the Jardiniere.

Jilt Jealous Jacks and Jills in a Jiffy!

Joust Judiciously with Jesuits.

Jump in Jalopies for Jubilant Jaunts.

Jitterbug in a Jonquil Jacket, a Juniper Jersey and a Jolly Jade Jumper.

Justify Jazz.

Keep Killjoys Kenneled.

Kiss Kittens and Kangaroos.

Kowtow in Kicky Kelly Kimonos and Kitschy Khaki Kepis.

Kay-o Kwashiorkor and Kalaazar.

Know Karma and Kindle Knowledge.

Kibitz with Khans and Kings.

Knight Kennedy, Kant and Keats.

Kid Kooks and Klutzes Kindly.

Kibosh Kazoos.

Lament Lambent Light and Lovely Landscapes Lost in Limbo.

Lounge Lazily along Lush Languid Lagoons and Lonesome Lapis Lakes Like a Little Lizard.

Lambada in Lavender Lamé Loungewear or Lacy Lime Leotards with Lilac Lupine in your Lapel.

Leap Lightly into Licit Lusty Liaisons.

Laud Leonardo, Lancelot and Longfellow.

Love Laudable Leigonniares with Lively Libidos!

Linger in Luxurious Lanais and Live Lavishly.

Labor at Legerdemain and Learn Local Lore.

Like Lutes.

Manufacture Marvelous Millinery Matching Magnolias, Marguerites and Marigolds with Multicolored Mantillas and Muster a Magnetic Motto and Mystic Mascot.

Make Mysterious Mauve Moccasins and a Mottled Maroon MuuMuu and Majestically March to a Mediterranean Marketplace by Moonlight.

Macerate Many Macaroons, Mixing Manners and Merriment at a Magnificent Millionaire's Mansion.

Masquerade at *Mardi Gras* as a Mythic Medieval Mummer and Mark Major Musical Minstrels and Minor Mediocre Mimes.

Make Much of Meeting Maverick Morpheus in a Misty Mindless Milieu.

Be Mesmerized by Manet and Monet, Marveling at Masterful Manifestations of Maestros.

Metempsychose Metamorphosing Magically and Master the Minuet and Mah Jong.

Memorize Multiple Motley Mammals — Mice, Mammoths, Marsupials, Martens, Muskrats, Monkeys, Mongooses, Mules and Mustangs.

Mark Mandolins.

Negotiate a Nifty New *Nom de plume* for your New-age Novel.

Neglect Nincompoops (Nitwits Notwithstanding!)

Nab a Neon Necktie in a Nanosecond and Nibble Nectarines Nonstop.

Nickname a Nubile Naughty Naiad "Natalie."

Note Numerology Nonchalantly.

Nap Naturally in Navy Nightclothes or Nest Nude, Needing Nothing.

Notify Neptune: No Nasty Narwhal Nets!

Notice Nirvana and Nascent Novas.

Nuke Noseharps.

Osculate with Otherworldly Oracles in Opulent Organic Orchards.

Outfit Others in Outlandish Orchid Organza Overalls and Observe.

Orate On Origami, Occasionally Offering Oodles Of Opinions, Otherwise Ordinary Options Often Obstruct Opportunity.

Obey an Occult Oath to Osiris.

Obtain an Outstanding Old Outrigger and Oar Outrageously Over the Ocean.

Obsess Omnisciently On Otherwise Ominous Occasions, Offending Obstinate Officials.

Orchestrate Osprey, Otters and Ocelots in an Orotund Overture.

Override Oafs and Ogres, Only Owning Obscure Oxymorons.

Oblige Oboes.

Passionately Participate in Pastlife Perusal and Ponder Peccadilloes Pursued in Previous Places.

Print a Playbill and Perform with Pensive Peacocks, Patient Pelicans and Piebald Palominos, Playing Peekaboo with Pusillanimous Peccaries.

Promote Premonitions, Promising to Participate in the Present.

Practice Panache, Persistently Proclaiming Plenitude.

Procure a Puce and Plum Parasol, a Pleated Pink Petticoat, a Pretty Painted Poppy Pinafore and Party with Prominent Pachyderms.

Park Pauline's Palanquin and Perch on a Palfrey, Propagating Pansies Profusely.

Purchase a Plaid Parka and Piqué Pantaloons, Proving you Perceive Proper Promenading.

Philosophize on Pertinent Passions, Preparing to Participate in a Practical Pilgrimage.

Prize Piccolos.

Quack Querulously.

Quote Quatrains.

Quaff Quinine.

Quarry Quartz.

Quiz Queens.

Qualify Quietly.

Quibble Quickly.

Question Quality.

Query Quartets.

Recruit Rubenesque Redheads to Rally 'Round the Rotunda, Romping Randily.

Relate *les Raisons d'être* of Rabelais and Racine to Random Republicans.

Romance Rowdy Rascals, Rendering Rogues Randy and Restless.

Regale Raconteurs with Racy Renditions of Rough and Ready Rodeos in the Rockies.

Reach Relentlessly for Rainbows and Rapture.

Reap the Respect of Random Regions, Retaining Restrained Reason.

Refurbish Rumpled Rose Reversible Rompers, Restoring your Reputation.

Rest, Relax and Reassure Relatives you Realize Reverie is Requisite.

Revere Recorders.

Sit Still by a Splashing Stream after a Spring Storm, Smelling Sagebrush and Softly Singing Simple Songs of Serendipity.

Seek Seclusion and Study the Summer Solstice, Sensing Spontaneous Spiritual Sanctification.

Sew a Smashing Short Sapphire Shantung Sarong, a Simple Silky Scarlet Satin Sash and a Sparkling Shiny Silver Samite Serape and Sashay Slowly Shoreward.

Select a Suitable Saraband and Shimmy, Slip, Slide, Shake, and Shuffle Showing Spontaneous Showmanship.

Summon Sun and Stars Sassily and See if they Show.

Sample Sauteed Shrimp with Saki Sauce, Salmon with Salsa, Scallops with Shallots and Sherry and other Salubrious Seafood, Sharing with Strong, Sensitive Sailors at Spectacular Seaside Sunset Serenades.

Sequester your Sylphlike Sister in a Shady Seraglio for the Summer; Send a Satchel with Samples of Scents, Sonnets and Sarsaparilla So She Senses your Sincerity.

Seek Someone Special for a Secret Seance at a Sylvan Shrine and Solicit Support for Something Sacred.

Squelch Sousaphones.

Talk Tactfully of Tawdry Tangos, Torrid Trysts and Tender *Têt à Têtes*.

Tease The Traditional about Tacky Tattoos and Tantalizing Taboos.

Try a Temporary Trance Technique, Thinking Tantric Thoughts.

Tailor Tasteful Turquoise Tasseled Tartans and Topaz Taffeta Toques and Transform Tatterdemalions To Talented Thespians.

Trim Thyself a Tonsure and Treasure Truth.

Trek To Tropical Tanganyika and Taste Tart Tomatoes and Tangy Tangelos under the Towering Tamarisks.

Thwack Tambourines, Telling Tales of Threatening Thunderclouds, Tremendous Tsunamis, and Terrifying Tempests Turning To Temperate Times in Tranquil Terrain.

Traipse Tentatively Through the Tourmaline Tidepools, Transfixed by Terrapins.

Tout Tubas.

Upgrade Umiaks.

Undertake Understanding Urdu.

Unfurl Ultramarine Umbrellas.

Uplift the Underprivileged.

Upset the Uppercrust.

Urge Utopia.

Uphold Ultimatums.

Underexpose Uvulas.

Unplug Ukuleles.

Vacate Violent Villages and Vamoose, Veiled on a Vermillion Velocipede.

Venerate Virgil, Van Gogh, Venus and Vicuñas.

Vitiate Vaguery Valiantly.

Vend Various Viands.

Veto Vain Voluminous Violet Velour Vestments.

Value Vocal Visionaries and Various Velvety Valentines.

Vex Villifiers of Voluptuous Vestal Virgins.

Vindicate Virile Vampires.

Vaunt Violas.

Wish for Wacky Wizards and Wonderful Waitresses.

Warily Ward Whales.

Waft from Weir to Welkin, Warbling Welsh War Whoops.

Wonder Where and When Wisdom Will be Welcome.

Weave a Wash-and-Wear Wool Wardrobe in Walnut and Woad.

Wolf Watermelon (With Wine) 'neath Weeping Willows and Wisteria Whenever you Want.

Worship Wild Warblers, Wonderful Wildflowers and Will-o-the-Wisps.

Wow Worrywarts With Walloons.

Whittle Woodwinds.

Xerox Xiphodons.

X-ray Xanthic Xemes.

Study the Xosa in the Xyst.

Enjoy Xylopyrography.

Visit Xenial Xenophobes at their Xenodochin.

Xerophage Xanthorhoea.

"X" out Xerifs.

Spend Xerafins on Xoanons.

X-rate Xylophones.

Yield Your Yarmulke to Yonder Yenta.

Yap of Yin and Yang over Yummy Yogurt.

Yawn at Yahoos and Yeggs.

Yelp if You're Yoked to a Yucca or a Yardarm.

Yank Your Yellow Yoyo in Yaounde or Yokohama.

Yaw Yuppie Yachts at Yuletide.

Yip at Yonkers Yokels and Young Yetis.

Yearn for Yearly Yoga with Yoda under Yggdrasil.

Yea, Yodelers!

Zap Zillions of Zany Zouaves in Zabras.

Zero in on Zen.

Zoom to the Zenith of a Ziggurat.

Study Zymurgy Zealously.

Zing Zechined Zombies with Zest.

Zounds! Zeitgeist?

Zima?

Zigzag on a Zephyr in a Zibeline Zeppelin.

Zoitolate Zithers.

*Dedicated
to
Diligently
Dabbling
in
Delightful
Daffiness!*

www.ingramcontent.com/pod-product-compliance
Lightning Source LLC
Chambersburg PA
CBHW040446080426
42451CB00024B/9